Wow!

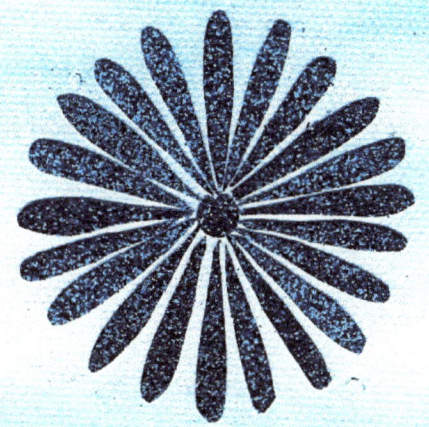

Carol A. Greene

Wow!

Copyright © 2023 by Carol A. Greene
All rights reserved

ISBN: 979-8-218-21447-0

Published by Carol A. Greene, Los Gatos, California 95033-8501
Printed in the United States of America.

All text, illustrations and characters in this book are copyrighted © 2023 by Carol A. Greene.

Author and illustrator: Carol A. Greene, Los Gatos, California 95033-8501.

Luanna K. Leisure, Little White Feather Graphic Artist and Independent Publisher, Campbell, California 95008.

To order additional books go to: www.lulu.com, Amazon.com, or Barnesandnoble.com

Website: www.carolgreene.com
Email: carol@carolgreene.com

I can hug teddy bears!

Wow!

Wow!

I can see hummingbirds feed!

SOUNDS OF THE OCEAN

Teaching hints:
1. Teach group the first part, so they'll know it for the end, then teach each group its part. Start directing in 4/4 time.

2. Start group 1, then bring in each group until all 5 groups are chanting.

3. Then start cutting groups.
Cut in this order: 3. gulls, 4. crows, 5. birds in the distance, 2. wings
As each group is cut, that group chants part 1 until the ocean is all that is heard. Then fade out to silence.

Group 1. (Whisper the sound of the ocean:)
       Wish………now…………(4 counts)   Wish…………..now…………..
       Wish………now…………(4 counts)   Wish…………..now…………..

Group 2. (Wings of sea birds)
       Th~~~~~~~~~~~~~~~~~~~~~~~~~~~(tongue vibrates) (8 counts)
       Th~~~~~~~~~~~~~~~~~~~~~~~~~~~(tongue vibrates)

Group 3. (Gulls--medium high pitch)
       uh uh uh ....(4 counts)   uh uh uh ....
       uh uh uh ....   uh uh uh ....

Group 4. (Crows scolding in a higher raspy pitch:)
       aw....... aw........(4 counts)   aw....... aw.......
       aw....... aw.......   aw....... aw.......

Group 5. (Birds in the distance--said quickly in the highest pitch, then whisper of the surf:)
       do it do it do it do it (4 counts)   shshshsh…………. (4 counts)
       do it do it do it do it (4 counts)   shshshsh…………. (4 counts)

I can make a mask!

BASIC VENTRILOQUISM

1. Hold your puppet shoulder level at your side with its eyes looking at the audience then you.
2. Lightly touch your teeth together and smile.
3. Look at your puppet to give the illusion that it is alive when it speaks and sings.
4. Give your puppet's voice a different quality and/or pitch from yours.
5. Open your puppet's mouth for each syllable, moving your thumb.
6. Speak slowly and punch the words.
7. Sound substitutions for the following letters:
    - F = th as in thin
    - V = th as in there
    - M = ng as in thing
    - W = oo-ah very quickly
    - Q = koo-ah very quickly
    - P = t or k
    - B = d or hard g
8. Take a deep breath, then slowly let it out as your puppet speaks. You will develop your diaphragm and project your voice when you do ventriloquism.
9. Ask your puppet questions, and have the puppet answer. It's amazing what your puppets will tell you!
10. Sing "Row, Row, Row Your Boat" with your puppet.
11. Lightly touch your lower lip, to feel mouth movement.
    Have fun practicing in the mirror!
    www.carolgreene.com/education/index/index.html

I can make Christmas ornaments!

Wow!

I like to go ride on a bike,
It's harder than riding a trike,
I try not to fall
Or hit a brick wall,
It's faster than taking a hike.

I wish I could soar through the sky,
Over the treetops I'd fly,
I'd giggle with glee,
I'd scream, "Look at me!"
Then spiral and spin way up high!

I can laugh at limericks!

An ice cream bar is a rare treat,
Especially outdoors in the heat,
Take care not to drip
When it touches your lip,
And don't let it drop in the street!

Limericks have five clever lines,
Lines 1, 2, and 5 always rhyme,
Line 4 rhymes with 3,
Just 2 beats you see,
We laugh on line 5 every time.

Wow!

I can blow bubbles!

GIANT BUBBLES

- 1 large bucket
- 6 cups of tap water
- ½ cup of Dawn dishwashing detergent
- 2 tablespoons of glycerin
- 2 sticks, 1 cotton string, and 1 or 2 heavy washers

- For best results, let the bubble solution rest for a few hours.
- To make the bubble wand, tie a long cotton string to each of the two sticks making a complete circle. Add the washers to the bottom of the circle before you tie a knot to the other stick.
- Put the bubble wand into the bubble solution. Then spread the wand out to make a circle to create a long bubble!

Wow!

I can lick an ice cream cone!

I can sing silly songs!

IN THE SWAMP

Say the chorus, say verse #1 twice, then repeat the chorus.
Say verse #2, repeat verse #1 and the chorus.
Continue in this way, adding a verse and repeating the previous verses until all seven verses have been said.
After the last chorus, loudly yell, "SWAMP MONSTER!" then scream!

Chorus:
In the swamp,   (Make two slurp-slurp sounds & shut fingers)
In the swamp,   (Make two slurp-slurp sounds & shut fingers)
We go squishy, squashy, squishy
In the swamp!   (Make two slurp-slurp sounds & shut fingers)

VERSES	MOTIONS
1. 'Gators chomp! (clap, clap)	(Stiff arms imitate moving mouth.)
2. Slithering snakes (sss, sss)	(Hands and arms move in a curve.)
3. Biting bugs (zzz, zzz)	(Fast pointing fingers attack head.)
4. Croaking frogs (ribbit, ribbit)	(Shrug shoulders.)
5. Howling wind! (whoo, whoo)	(Arms make wind crossing face.)
6. Pouring rain! (sh, sh)	(Fingers wiggle as raised arms fall.)
7. Clashing thunder!	(Feet quickly stomp. 8X)
8. SWAMP MONSTER! (scream)	(Hold arms up.)

Wow!

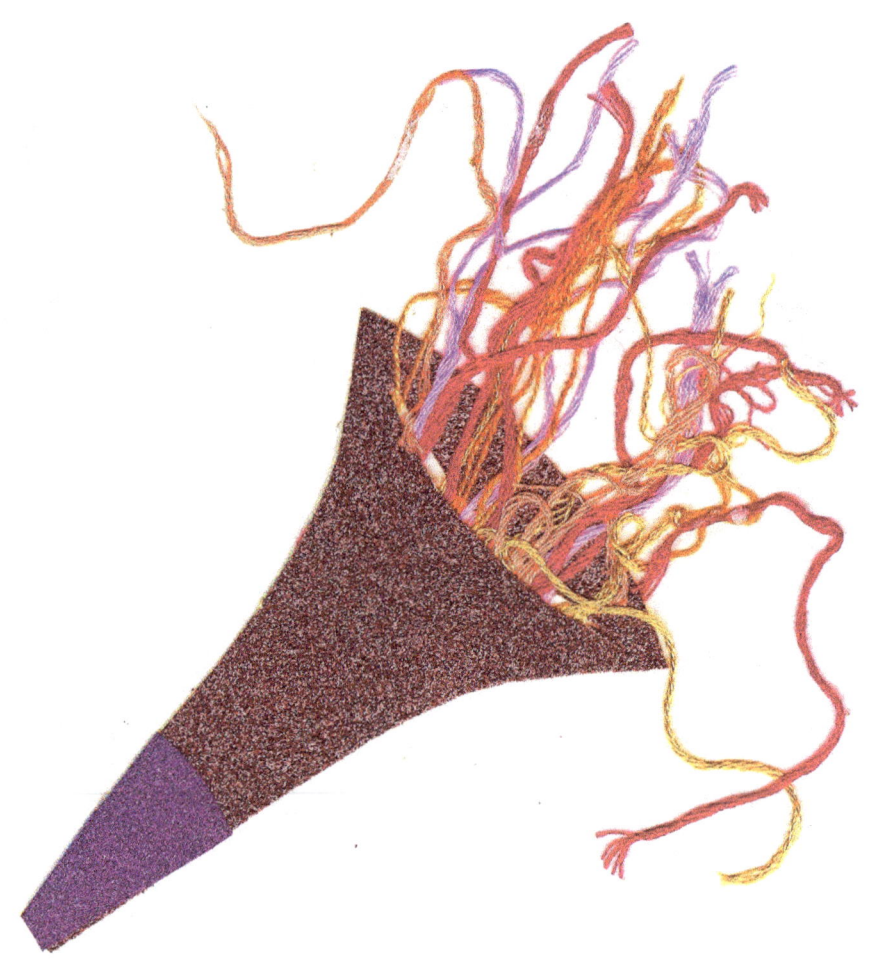

I can celebrate!

Wow!

I can do it!

You can do it too!

We can do it!

About the Author
Carol A. Greene

When Carol was a university student, she earned all of her expenses as a piano teacher and as a ventriloquist, magician, and clown for children's birthday parties. She graduated with a degree in elementary education. She taught for 33 years, first as an intermediate classroom teacher, then as a Creative Arts and Orff Schulwerk Traveling Specialist. Her puppets were her assistants. She also was a scout leader.

She has traveled with family, puppets and friends to six continents, including much of the United States. She loves the beauty of the ocean, waterfalls, and mountains. She lives in California. She and her husband have a son, daughter, and granddaughter.

She believes that we can all accomplish our dreams. You can do it too!

www.ingramcontent.com/pod-product-compliance
Lightning Source LLC
Chambersburg PA
CBHW041637040426
42449CB00022B/3493